Follow A River

by J. Matteson Claus

PEARSON
Scott Foresman

DK

What You Already Know

The Earth is made of three main layers. The crust, or outer layer, is about 37 km (23 miles) thick. The mantle, the next layer under the crust, is about 2,900 km (1,800 miles) thick. The core is the innermost layer.

Magma is hot, thick, melted rock. It is under high pressure because of its great depth and underground gases. Magma that reaches near the surface flows more easily. It erupts through areas of weakness in the Earth's crust. These openings are called volcanoes.

Magma that has reached the Earth's surface is called lava. When the lava hardens it forms a new portion of the Earth's crust.

Volcanic eruptions release lava from underground.

Landforms can change due to weathering. Weathering is any action that breaks rocks into smaller pieces. When weathered material is moved, the process is called erosion. The wind can erode landforms. It picks up weathered materials and blows them to a different place. Water, glaciers, and gravity can also cause erosion.

There are many forces that can change the form of the Earth. Included in those forces of change are the Earth's rivers. Rivers are pretty to look at and fun to swim in. But they also change the landscape in a dramatic way.

What is a river?

A river is a waterway that flows across land. Some rivers are calm. They flow slowly and gently across the land. Other rivers flow quickly, forming waterfalls and rapids. Whether a river roars or drifts depends on the shape of the land it flows over.

Each river has its own path. It begins at a source, such as a spring, lake, or glacier. Most rivers end when they reach the ocean, or flow into another river or lake.

Rivers are fed by tributaries. Tributaries are smaller streams that flow into rivers. They increase a river's size. Rivers can powerfully reshape the land on their journey to the ocean.

Rivers are an important part of the water cycle. They collect the Earth's water and transport it to different places.

Rivers do more than just change the land and move water. They provide transportation, food, water, and energy. The fertile land along riverbanks allows farmers to grow food for a large part of the world's population. Without rivers, ships couldn't transport people and goods inland to and from the sea. Rivers are crucial to life on Earth in many different ways.

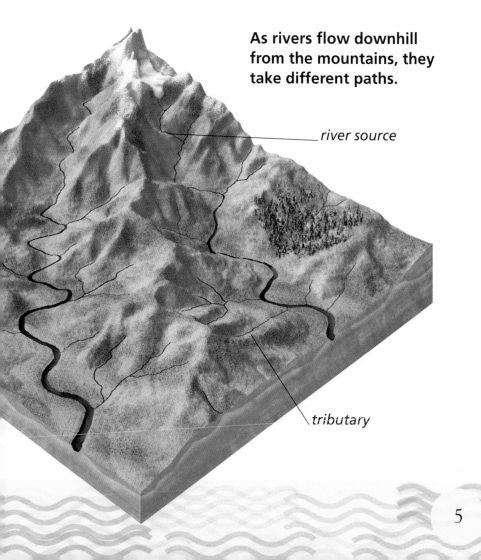

As rivers flow downhill from the mountains, they take different paths.

river source

tributary

At the Source

Rivers form when water flows from a higher place to a lower place. Picture snow melting from a mountaintop. Some of the water is absorbed by the ground. As the melting continues, the ground can't absorb additional water as well. The excess water collects in puddles. As the puddles grow, the water starts to trickle down the mountain. This trickle of water is called runoff. Runoff collects to form a small stream, or rivulet. Farther down the mountain, several rivulets come together, forming a new river, or flowing into an existing river.

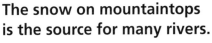

**The snow on mountaintops
is the source for many rivers.**

Many rivers flow quickly right at their start. They can pick up energy if more rivers flow into them.

Different rivers begin in different places. Some begin at springs. Others form from lakes, melting glaciers, snow, or rain.

Young rivers grow rapidly and change quickly. When they have a swift flow, they often carve out valleys with steep, narrow walls. Valleys create paths for tributaries to flow into young rivers. Young rivers grow with each added tributary. Melting snow or heavy rain also makes them grow. Young rivers tend to create waterfalls and rapids as they flow over and around the rocks that are in their path.

The same sources that form new rivers also keep existing rivers flowing. Without a steady supply of water, rivers can dry up. Some rivers, called seasonal rivers, are dry for some months of the year.

Moving Downstream

Rivers usually flow rapidly when the ground they flow over is steep. They usually flow slowly when the ground they flow over is level. Rapidly flowing rivers carve out valleys with high, narrow walls. Rivers that move slowly create valleys with wider and more gently sloped sides.

The ground a river flows over also affects the size and shape of a valley. A river flowing down a mountain made of hard rock may form a very steep valley, or gorge. A river on softer rock can become very fast when it flows over a place with harder rock. When this happens, rapids are formed.

As the land around a river levels out, the river's loops and bends become larger and larger.

When the surface of the land is level, rivers form many curves, loops, or bends. This gives them a snakelike appearance. Sometimes the river's flow will cut away at the sides of a curve. This forms a loop in the river. Eventually, this loop will become completely separated from the rest of the river. When that happens, the loop becomes a small, curved lake. Such lakes are known as oxbow lakes. By cutting off loops, rivers take more direct paths to their destinations.

Oxbow lakes are formed when rivers change directions.

Oxbow lake

Erosion and Sediment

Rivers are always reshaping the landforms around them. Sometimes rivers reshape the land a lot. The Grand Canyon was formed by the Colorado River. The canyon is 227 miles long and more than a mile deep! But rivers are also constantly reshaping the land in ways we don't even see.

As rivers flow, they rub against the bottom and sides of the land. Erosion is when this rubbing picks up small pieces of rock and soil. These materials are called sediment. The river carries eroded sediment downstream. As the sediment is carried downstream, it also scrapes the bottoms and sides of the land, causing more erosion. This same erosion is what began forming the Grand Canyon 10 million years ago.

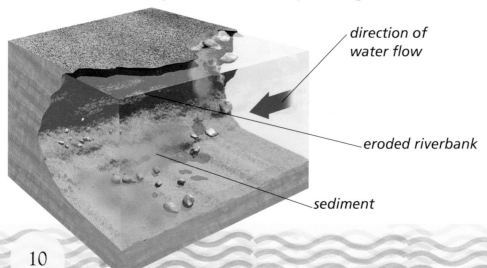

direction of water flow

eroded riverbank

sediment

the Colorado River

Rivers erode valleys in different ways. A river can create caverns and caves by eroding limestone. Waterfalls can form when a river flowing over hard rock passes over softer rock. The river will carve out the softer rock, forming a slope the water falls over. Oxbow lakes and rapids are also formed by erosion.

The amount of erosion caused by a river also depends on its speed. A slower-moving river can carry less sediment than a faster-moving river. A river with less sediment will cause less erosion because there will be less material scraping the riverbed.

waterfall

Deposition

While erosion wears land away, deposition builds it up. Deposition is when sediment from erosion is carried by the river and placed, or deposited, in another area of the river. Sometimes erosion and deposition take place on opposite banks of the same river bend. At other times, the sediment will travel all the way to the mouth of the river. There it will probably be deposited in the river's delta.

How far sediment travels depends on how heavy it is. Heavier sediment will be deposited before lighter sediment. Because of this, many riverbeds are rocky near their source and sandy at their end.

The river deposits sediment on the inner bends while eroding the outer bends.

River islands form from sediment deposits that build up over time.

Rivers also deposit lots of sediment when they flood. Floods are usually the result of heavy rain or rapidly melting snow. The extra water from floods raises rivers' water levels. This causes rivers to overflow their banks. During floods, rivers deposit sediment on the land surrounding the river. This area is known as a floodplain. Some rivers, such as the Mississippi River, flood every year. These rivers have very fertile floodplains. People often live and grow crops on floodplains.

Some rivers can also create islands by depositing sediment on shallow parts of the river bottom. These islands force the river to flow through separate channels. This is called a braided river.

River's End

Some rivers' journeys end upon reaching the sea. There, a delta often forms. Deltas are formed as sediment is deposited at the mouth of the river. As the sediment builds up, the river is broken up into smaller channels. These channels empty out into the sea. Deltas are often fan-shaped, but can be other shapes depending on the river and the land around it. They are some of the most fertile areas in the world. After its long flow across the Egyptian desert, the Nile River forms one of the world's most famous and fertile deltas where it meets the Mediterranean Sea.

The Nile Delta creates a fan-shaped patch of green in the harsh Egyptian desert.

Nile River

Rivers play an important role in supporting life on Earth. Next time you pass a river, look at the area surrounding it. Note how its flowing water has changed the landscape. Rivers create habitats that animals can live in. Sediment deposited by rivers makes the ground fertile so people can grow crops. They provide water for farming and for drinking. Some of the first human civilizations began next to rivers. The Nile allowed ancient Egyptians to thrive in the desert. They are also natural pathways for shipping and travel. Without rivers, we'd be left high and dry!

Glossary

delta   a deposit of sand or soil that forms at the mouth of a river

deposition   process of laying down sediment from erosion

oxbow lake   a lake created when a section of a river is cut off from the rest of the river

rivulets   small streams

runoff   the portion of precipitation that isn't absorbed by the land and instead flows across the top of the land

sediment   materials carried and deposited by water

tributaries   streams feeding a larger stream, lake, or river

What did you learn?

1. What are the possible sources of a river?

2. When a river erodes the landscape, what are the possible results?

3. What is an oxbow lake? How is it formed?

4. **Writing** in Science In this book you have read about the life of a river. Write to explain how a river changes the landscape using the processes of erosion and deposition. Use examples from the book.

5. **Sequence** Several things must happen for a river to form. Place these things in order: Runoff begins to trickle down the mountain; the young river grows with each added tributary; snow melts from the top of a mountain; several runoffs flow together to form a small stream, or rivulet.

Science

Genre	Comprehension Skill	Text Features	Science Content
Nonfiction	Sequence	• Captions • Diagrams • Call Outs • Glossary	Changes on Earth

Scott Foresman Science 3.8